T0145170

BETSY,
THE CROSS-BEAK CHICKEN

A True Story

By Rina Sartiano-Gibbons

AuthorHouse™
1663 Liberty Drive
Bloomington, IN 47403
www.authorhouse.com
Phone: 833-262-8899

Because of the dynamic nature of the Internet, any web addresses or links contained in this book may have changed
since publication and may no longer be valid. The views expressed in this work are solely those of the author and do not
necessarily reflect the views of the publisher, and the publisher hereby disclaims any responsibility for them.

Any people depicted in stock imagery provided by Getty Images are models,
and such images are being used for illustrative purposes only.
Certain stock imagery © Getty Images.

This book is printed on acid-free paper.

ISBN: 978-1-6655-6128-0 (sc)
ISBN: 978-1-6655-6127-3 (e)

Library of Congress Control Number: 2022910495

Print information available on the last page.

Published by AuthorHouse 06/07/2022

authorHOUSE®

Betsy didn't look much like her five feathered friends.

There was

Martha

Abigail

Dolly

Harriet

Eliza

And then there was Betsy, the Cross-Beak Chicken!

Betsy wasn't always unusual.

When she arrived at her new home and met Farm Girl for the first time, Betsy looked just like the tiny chicks who traveled with her, in a special mailing box.

But as Betsy grew, something odd happened to her! Her upper and lower beak began growing in different directions! Betsy's beak was growing topsy-turvy, and that was not good news for a young chicken.

It would be hard for her to use a topsy-turvy beak to do the things chickens must, like pecking her food and preening her feathers.

Farm Girl tried to help Betsy by gluing metal pegs, wrapped with rubber bands, around her beak. She thought it would work like the braces kids wear, to straighten their crooked teeth.

But the metal pegs and rubber bands did not work very well on Betsy's beak. She could barely open it enough to peck her food, guzzle water, or even say "cluck!"

Farm Girl saw it was now time to consult a chicken expert. So with Betsy settled in her safe-bird carrier, Farm Girl set off for Doctor Pullum's All Creatures Clinic.

Farm Girl waited as Dr. Pullum took a good long look at Betsy's unusual beak.

"Hmm. Oh my. Yes, indeed. Well this little chicken has a clear case of lateral beak deviation."

"In other words," Dr. Pullum said, "Betsy is a special cross-beak chicken. And she has a *good* chance of growing up strong and healthy, with a little help."

Betsy, the Cross-Beak Chicken, went home to her flock in the chicken yard. Every day, Farm Girl brought her a bowl of soft, mushy chicken gruel, so that Betsy could scoop it up with her crooked beak.

Now that she could eat more easily, Betsy grew strong and healthy. She was finally able to dust herself with dirt, scratch the ground for bugs, and play with her flock mates in the chicken yard.

Sometimes, Farm Girl gave Betsy a warm, soapy bath and would blow-dry her feathers. It was hard to preen and stay clean with a cross beak.

One day, Farm Girl placed an old mirror in the chicken yard, for the flock to enjoy.

Martha, Abigail, Dolly, Harriet, and Eliza were delighted with their reflections. They did a lot of wing flapping, bobbing, clucking, and posing in front of the shiny glass.

All the hens enjoyed the old mirror, all except Betsy. Unlike her flock mates, who saw Betsy's cross beak every day, *she* had never seen a chicken beak that looked quite like *hers*! At least, not until now, when Betsy saw her own image in the mirror!

She was surprised and alarmed by her own reflection. So Farm Girl gently lifted Betsy onto her lap and soothed her ruffled feathers.

"I love you Betsy Cross-Beak," she cooed. "You're one fine chicken, just the way you are."

Autumn turned to winter, spring came to an end, and finally, it was summer. For many months, Farm Girl had cared for the six growing chickens.

Now they were ready to do their job.

It was a wonderful moment when, one by one, each young hen took a turn in the nesting box and laid her first egg!

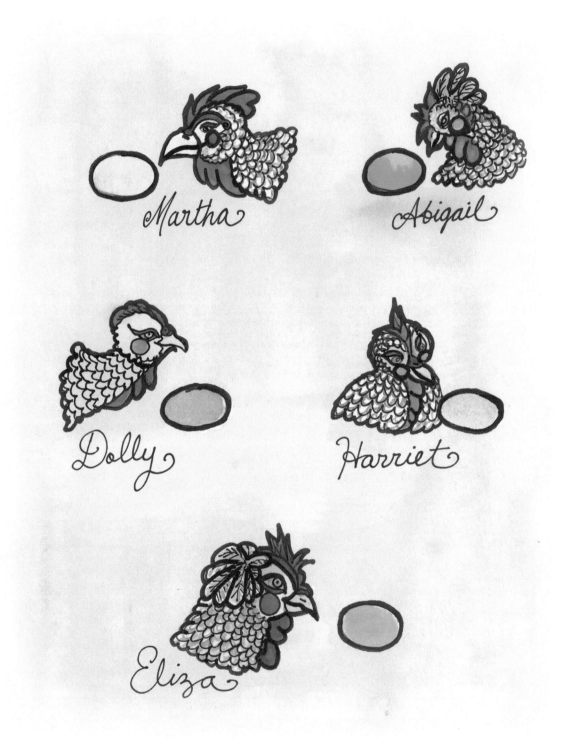

Some laid pale blue eggs and some laid milk chocolate-colored eggs.

As the weeks passed, only one chicken had not laid her first egg. Betsy was over eight months old and still had no eggs to show or share.

Farm Girl knew it could take longer for Betsy to lay an egg. A cross-beak chicken needed a little more time to grow.

But this did not matter to Farm Girl. She knew Betsy would do her job when she was ready! And she cherished Betsy just as much as she did Martha, Abigail, Dolly, Harriet, and Eliza.

Then one late-summer morning, the sky looked especially blue. Farm Girl strolled into the chicken yard, to feed the flock and collect their freshly laid eggs.

And there, beaming up from the nesting box, was a proud Betsy Cross-Beak, snuggling the most perfect violet-blue egg ever seen!

That day, the chicken yard felt different. The hens were happy that Betsy had begun to lay eggs of her own.

Betsy was a special cross-beak chicken. In the years to come, she laid many beautiful eggs and became an important part of her flock's pecking order. She proved that she could do her job and live happily, even though her topsy-turvy beak made growing up a little harder.

Farm Girl continued to love and cherish Betsy the Cross-Beak Chicken, probably even a little bit *more* than she did Martha, Abigail, Harriet, Dolly, and Eliza!

Author Biography

Rina S. Gibbons started her career as an intelligence officer, living in San Francisco, California. Eventually, her family took precedence, and she reared her children fulltime, while pursuing a career as a private investigator, small business owner, early-childhood teacher and tireless school volunteer. Once her children left home, Ms. Gibbons and her husband moved to a small farm in Sonoma, California where she raised chickens, ducks, and sheep. Her true experiences with a handicapped chicken led to the sweet and heartwarming story about Betsy, the Cross-Beaked Chicken. Ms. Gibbons currently lives in New Jersey with her husband, John, a Brussels Griffon named Gatsby, and Clara, a Great Pyrenees.

Printed in the United States
by Baker & Taylor Publisher Services